How Do They Make That?

Fractions, Decimals, and Percents

Lori Barker

Consultants

Pamela Dase, M.A.Ed.
National Board Certified Teacher

Barbara Talley, M.S.
Texas A&M University

Publishing Credits

Dona Herweck Rice, *Editor-in-Chief*
Robin Erickson, *Production Director*
Lee Aucoin, *Creative Director*
Timothy J. Bradley, *Illustration Manager*
Sara Johnson, M.S.Ed., *Senior Editor*
Aubrie Nielsen, M.S.Ed., *Associate Education Editor*
Jennifer Kim, M.A.Ed., *Associate Education Editor*
Neri Garcia, *Senior Designer*
Stephanie Reid, *Photo Editor*
Rachelle Cracchiolo, M.S.Ed., *Publisher*

Image Credits

Teacher Created Materials

5301 Oceanus Drive
Huntington Beach, CA 92649-1030
http://www.tcmpub.com
ISBN 978-1-4333-3453-5
© 2012 Teacher Created Materials, Inc.

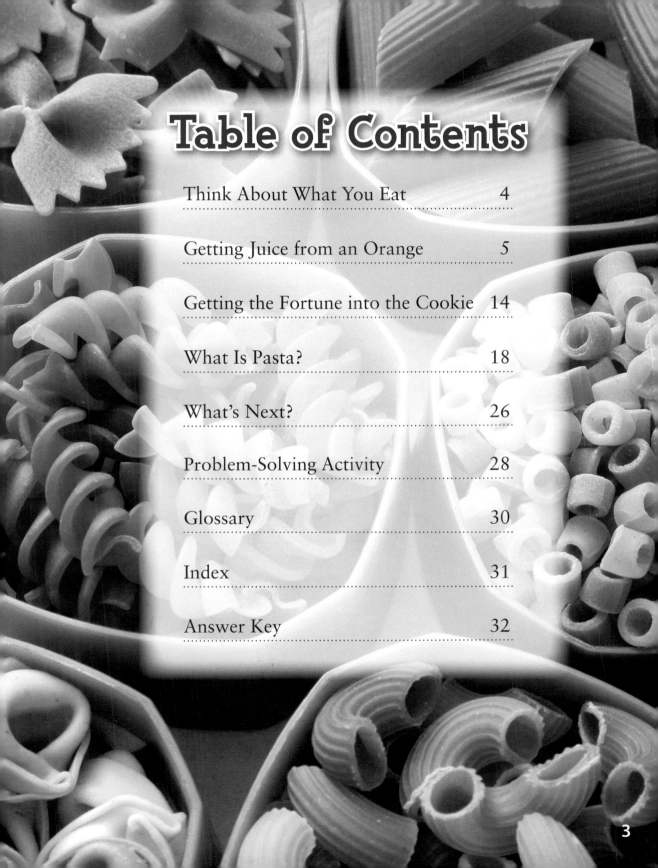

Table of Contents

Think About What You Eat

What did you eat yesterday? Did you have any juice, cereal, or canned vegetables? Was anything homemade or purchased from a grocery store? In the aisles of a grocery store there are cans of soup, packages of noodles, bottles of juice, boxes of cereal, cartons of ice cream, and countless other food items. Where does all that food come from? How is it all made?

Large grocery stores, also called *supermarkets*, carry anywhere from 15,000 to 60,000 different products on their shelves.

Getting Juice from an Orange

Making fresh orange juice can be as simple as squeezing an orange. But many people buy containers of juice. Either way, orange juice starts with oranges.

Oranges grow on trees in groves. When they are ready to be **harvested**, they are usually picked by hand. If a box holds about 75 to 80 oranges, the youngest trees (1–3 years old) tend to **yield** just over one box. Mature trees that are over 24 years old tend to yield about five boxes.

Boxes of Oranges Produced by Five Trees

You can use addition to find the total number of boxes of oranges produced by 5 trees.

$$\begin{array}{r} 1.850 \text{ boxes} \\ 2.500 \text{ boxes} \\ 4.000 \text{ boxes} \\ 3.125 \text{ boxes} \\ + 2.750 \text{ boxes} \\ \hline 14.225 \text{ boxes} \end{array}$$

Brazil and the United States are the top two growers of oranges in the world. The orange juice from these two countries makes up 85% of the orange juice produced in the world.

Always add or subtract digits from the same place value. Remember to line up the decimals if you write the numbers in a column.

Trucks move oranges from the fields to packing centers. Imagine a truck that holds 47.2 thousand pounds of oranges. Eight trucks could hold a little under 400 thousand pounds. About 68.5 million tons of oranges are produced each year. It takes a lot of trucks to move all those oranges!

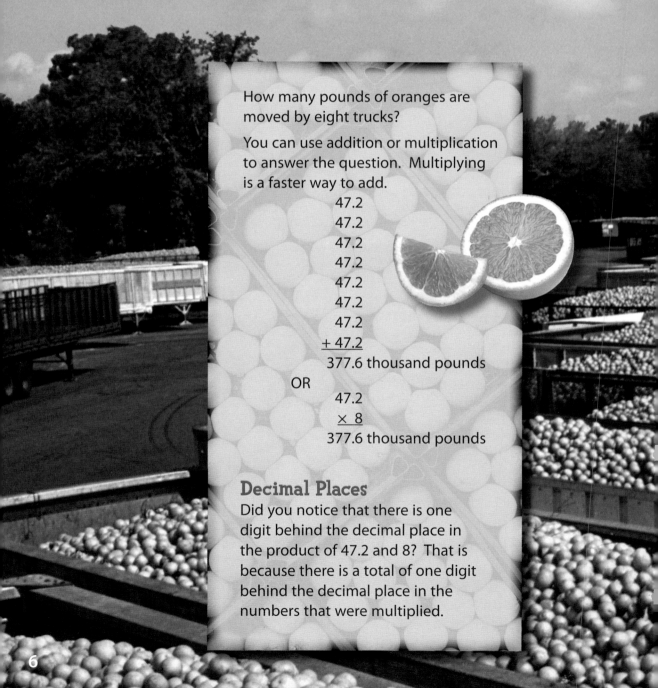

How many pounds of oranges are moved by eight trucks?

You can use addition or multiplication to answer the question. Multiplying is a faster way to add.

47.2
47.2
47.2
47.2
47.2
47.2
47.2
+ 47.2
377.6 thousand pounds

OR

47.2
× 8
377.6 thousand pounds

Decimal Places

Did you notice that there is one digit behind the decimal place in the product of 47.2 and 8? That is because there is a total of one digit behind the decimal place in the numbers that were multiplied.

Of course, the whole orange cannot be eaten or used for juice. For some types of oranges, about 73 **percent** (73%) of the orange is **edible** (ED-uh-buhl). The rest of the orange is the rind and the seeds. If the weight of an orange is known, the weight of the edible portion can be found.

Weight of an orange: 125 grams

To find the weight of the edible portion, use the following expression: 125×0.73 (*0.73 is* **equivalent** *to 73%. To change a percent to a decimal, divide by 100. This moves the decimal point two places to the left.*)

Multiplying Decimals

Step 1: Remove the decimals. Multiply. $125 \times 73 = 9{,}125$

Step 2: Count the number of decimal places in the **factors** (2 decimal places). $125 \times 0.\underline{73}$

Step 3: Place the decimal point in the product. 91.25

Edible portion: $125 \times 0.73 = 91.25$ grams

LET'S EXPLORE MATH

a. Three samples of oranges are gathered. The samples weigh 12.43 pounds, 18.5 pounds, and 8.77 pounds. What is the total weight of the samples?

b. An inspector examines six samples each day. Each sample includes 100–150 oranges and weighs 37.2 pounds. How many pounds of oranges does she inspect each day?

Oranges are sorted at a packing center. Some are sold as whole fruit and some are used to make juice. The oranges must be washed. Damaged oranges must be pulled out. Workers carefully inspect samples of oranges to make sure they meet quality standards.

Imagine an inspector examines 20 oranges. Thirty percent of the oranges are damaged. How many oranges are damaged?

Thirty percent (30%) is the same as 3 out of 10. Since there are two groups of 10 in 20, we find that 3 out of each group are damaged, for a total of 6 damaged oranges. Thirty percent of 20 is 6.

We can also find the answer by multiplying 20 by 30%.
Convert the percent to a decimal and multiply:
20 x 0.3 = 6

A machine washes oranges at a factory.

The oranges that will be used for juice are sent on to a juice **extraction** (ik-STRAK-shuhn) facility. There is more than one method for extracting juice from oranges. One involves forcing the oranges though a blade that cuts them in half. Then rubber suction cups hold each half while the juice is taken out. In another method, two metal cups hold the whole orange. While in the cups, the peel is removed and the juice is pushed through tiny holes and into a tube that is attached to one of the cups.

Juice extractors are designed to take out the juice without mixing in too much of the oil from the peel. The oil can have a bitter taste.

After juice is extracted from oranges, it is passed through a screen in order to remove all the pulp and seeds. Some orange juice is sold with pulp and some is sold without pulp. If the orange juice will be sold with pulp, the pulp has to be added back in before the juice is put into a carton or bottle.

There are hundreds of **varieties** (vuh-RAHY-i-teez) of oranges. Common varieties used for juice include navel and Valencia oranges. Commercial orange juices are often made with more than one variety of orange. This helps juice manufacturers (man-yuh-FAK-cher-erz) create the exact flavor they need to make their juice special.

Navel oranges get their name from what looks like a belly button at their **apex**. This "navel" is actually a second, tiny orange. This tiny twin orange does not fully develop, but its small sections can be found inside the larger orange.

LET'S EXPLORE MATH

Suppose you have two oranges of different varieties. One weighs 88.2 grams. The second one weighs 75% more than the first one. Follow the instructions to find the weight of the second orange. Problems **a** and **b** use one method of solving the problem. Problem **c** uses a second method.

a. Calculate 88.2 x 0.75. This is the difference in the weight of the two oranges.

b. Add your answer for problem **a** to 88.2 to find the weight of the second orange.

c. Multiply 88.2 by 1.75 to find the weight of the heavier orange. (*Tip:* A 75% increase is the same as 175% of the original amount.)

d. Your answers for problems **b** and **c** should be the same. Explain why these answers are the same.

e. A third orange weighs 48% more than the first one. How much does it weigh? Round your answer to the nearest tenth.

The Juice Is Out! Now What?

In many cases, the juice is concentrated (KON-suhn-trey-tid) after it is filtered. That means that the taste of the juice is strengthened because the water is removed.

While in a **vacuum**, the juice is heated with steam. It reaches a temperature of 208.4°F (98°C). The water is then forced to evaporate. When finished, the juice lowers to a temperature of 113°F (45°C). The juice is then moved to a flash cooler where it is quickly cooled to 55.4°F (13°C). The concentrate is then frozen and shipped all over the world.

concentrated orange juice

Most juice that is sold ready-to-drink comes from concentrated juice. Frozen concentrated juice can be kept for much longer than fresh juice. It can also be stored and shipped much more cheaply.

In order to make concentrated orange juice ready to drink, the concentrate is thawed. Then water is added to **dilute** (dih-LOOT) the concentrate.

Usually many different batches of concentrate are used to create the perfect juice blend. The right blend is determined through careful testing and analysis.

A lot of the orange juice sold at the grocery store comes from concentrate. Fresh orange juice is usually labeled "not-from-concentrate."

LET'S EXPLORE MATH

Alyssa is watching the numbers fall on a thermometer as the juice is in the flash cooler. She notices the temperature is 110°F. Moments later she notices that the temperature has dropped by 40%.

a. By how many degrees has the temperature dropped?

b. What is the new temperature of the juice?

c. By how many degrees would the temperature have dropped if it had decreased by 60%?

Getting the Fortune into the Cookie

If you have eaten at a Chinese restaurant, you may have been served a fortune cookie for dessert. If you crack open a fortune cookie, you will likely find some words of wisdom, some Chinese characters, or a list of lucky numbers printed on a little slip of paper. But how does that "fortune" get inside the cookie? There are several factories that make these crispy cookies for the world to enjoy.

The Birthplace of the Fortune Cookie

Fortune cookies were invented in San Francisco, California, in the early 1900s. They are served in Chinese restaurants in many countries around the world, but are not really popular in China.

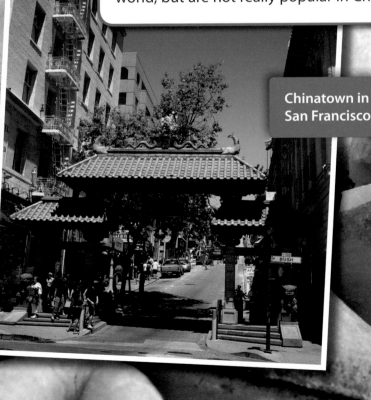

Chinatown in San Francisco

First, the cookie batter is made. This is usually a combination of sugar, oil, flour, eggs, water, and food coloring. The batter is mixed well. Next, the batter is poured into thin circles, like small pancakes. Then the disks of batter go into a hot oven to bake for about one minute.

A batch of fortune cookie batter weighs 493.5 pounds. Of the batter, 98.7 pounds is sugar. Divide the pounds of sugar by the pounds of batter, then multiply by 100 to find the percent of the batter that is sugar.

$$
\begin{array}{r}
0.2 \\
493.5\,\overline{\smash{)}98.7.0} \\
-98\ 7\ 0 \\
\hline
0
\end{array}
$$

Notice that we move the decimal in both the **divisor** and the **dividend** so that we can divide by a whole number.

$$
\begin{array}{r}
100 \\
\times\ 0.2 \\
\hline
20.0
\end{array}
$$

The batter is 20% sugar.

Converting a Decimal to a Percent

Moving the decimal point two places to the right is the same as multiplying by 100. When we change a decimal to a percent, we are showing what part of 100 it is.

When the flat cookie comes out of the oven, it is not given any time to cool. The "fortune" paper is placed on top of the soft cookie, and it is quickly folded into the famous fortune cookie shape. This can be done by hand, but in large factories this is done by a machine. Steal prongs push the cookie over a steal rod to fold the cookie into shape.

A worker folds fortune cookies.

Words of Wisdom

A factory may have over 5,000 different messages that are used in its fortune cookies. Originally, the "fortunes" were Chinese **proverbs** (PRAW-vurbz). Today, they are usually words of advice, positive predictions, or funny messages.

After the cookies cool and harden, they are packaged in plastic wrappers. The cookies are checked and broken ones are rejected before they are boxed and shipped. Over three billion fortune cookies are made each year around the world. The largest fortune cookie factory in the world is in Brooklyn, New York. It produces over four million cookies each day!

LET'S EXPLORE MATH

a. A fortune cookie factory produces 8,750 fortune cookies each day. If there are 350 cookies in each box, what percent of the cookies is in each box?

b. Another factory produces 393.3 kilograms of cookies each day. On Tuesday, 23.4 kilograms of cookies were damaged and rejected. What percent of the cookies were rejected on Tuesday? Round your answer to the hundredths place.

What Is Pasta?

Pasta is a popular food in many cultures and countries throughout the world. Pasta comes in all shapes, sizes, and colors. The most famous varieties of pasta come from Italy. Dried pastas are sold in most grocery stores, but fresh pastas can be made at home and in restaurants.

A chef prepares $5\frac{5}{6}$ pounds of spaghetti, $5\frac{1}{2}$ pounds of penne (PEN-ey), and $3\frac{3}{4}$ pounds of macaroni.

To find the total amount of pasta he made, add the mixed numbers.

Step 1: Find a common denominator. Make it the **least common denominator (LCD)** if possible.

$5\frac{5}{6} + 5\frac{1}{2} + 3\frac{3}{4}$

$5\frac{}{12} + 5\frac{}{12} + 3\frac{}{12}$

Step 2: Find equivalent fractions.

$5\frac{10}{12} + 5\frac{6}{12} + 3\frac{9}{12}$

Step 3: Add the whole numbers and add the fractions. Remember that when adding fractions, add only the numerators. The denominators stay the same.

$13\frac{25}{12}$

Step 4: Simplify the **improper fraction**. Divide the numerator by the denominator to get a mixed number.

$13 + 2\frac{1}{12}$

Step 5: Add the whole numbers and write the final answer as a mixed number.

$15\frac{1}{12}$ pounds

Finding the Least Common Denominator (LCD)

First, list **multiples** of each different denominator. Stop when you find a multiple that they all share. This is your LCD.

2: 2, 4, 6, 8, 10, ⑫
4: 4, 8, ⑫
6: 6, ⑫

Did You Know?
Pasta almost doubles in weight when cooked.

Pasta is often made from milled durum (DOOR-uhm) wheat. Semolina (sem-uh-LEE-nuh) comes from the heart, or **endosperm** (EN-duh-spurm), of durum wheat. Semolina is found in many brands and types of pasta. Sometimes pasta is made with only semolina and water. Sometimes other ingredients are added, such as egg solids, vegetable juices, herbs, and spices. These ingredients give flavor to the pasta.

LET'S EXPLORE MATH

a. Laura works in a grain mill. She makes sure that the semolina is of good quality before it is sent to be made into pasta. She worked three days last week. She worked $8\frac{3}{4}$ hours the first day, $7\frac{1}{2}$ hours the second day, and $8\frac{1}{4}$ hours the third day. How many total hours did she work that week?

b. How many hours did Laura work in one day if she was scheduled for $7\frac{2}{3}$ hours but had to leave $2\frac{1}{2}$ hours early?

Making Pasta

How do pasta makers know how much of the additional ingredients to add to the semolina and water? That question is answered with plenty of trial-and-error and taste testing.

The first step in making flavored pasta is to make sure that all of the ingredients are ready to use. Then the ingredients are mixed together to create the dough. The dough is tasted, and the best-tasting ones are used to create unique recipes.

Simplifying Fractions

To simplify a fraction, divide the numerator and the denominator by their **greatest common factor (GCF)**. When a fraction is in **simplest form**, the GCF of the numerator and denominator is 1.

A tray of pasta dough is divided into 15 portions for taste testing. $\frac{2}{3}$ of the tray has vegetable juices added. $\frac{2}{5}$ of the tray has herbs blended in. To find how many portions have both vegetable juices and herbs, we need to multiply $\frac{2}{3}$ by $\frac{2}{5}$. When we multiply these fractions we get $\frac{4}{15}$. So $\frac{4}{15}$ of the pasta dough has both vegetable juices and herbs.

v h	v h	v	v	v
v h	v h	v	v	v
h	h			

v = vegetable juices   h = herbs

$$\frac{2}{3} \times \frac{2}{5} = \frac{2 \times 2}{3 \times 5} = \frac{4}{15}$$

Pasta dough is formed into many different shapes and sizes. Long pasta is sometimes formed into strings or ribbons. Short pasta can be formed in the shape of shells, spirals, stars, bows, or wheels.

Pasta dough is a little less than $\frac{1}{3}$ water.
Think of 600 pounds of dough. Since $\frac{1}{3}$ of 600 is 200, about 200 pounds of the dough would be water.

Pasta that is mass-produced is made with the help of machines and computers.

Extrusion (ik-STROO-zhuhn) is a common method used for shaping pasta, especially short pasta. Mixed dough is pushed through a chamber where it passes through a brass mold. The shape of the mold determines the shape of the pasta. The pasta dough passes through the mold, and a machine cuts it to the preferred size.

After being shaped, the soft pasta needs to dry. It is first pre-dried which helps make sure that the pasta does not stick together. Then it is more fully dried so that the moisture in the pasta goes down to about 12.5 percent.

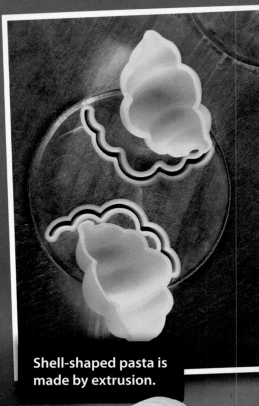

Shell-shaped pasta is made by extrusion.

Did You Know?
The countries that produce the most pasta are Italy and the United States.

LET'S EXPLORE MATH

One recipe for a small pasta salad calls for $\frac{2}{3}$ ounce of pasta.

a. Determine the amount of pasta needed for three-fourths of a recipe.

b. Determine the amount of pasta needed for a double recipe.

c. Determine the amount of pasta needed to increase the recipe $2\frac{3}{4}$ times.

d. Add your answer for problem **a** to your answer for problem **b**. How does this sum compare with your answer for problem **c**?

Proper drying is important. If the pasta dries too fast, cracks can develop. But if the pasta dries too slowly, it can spoil or mold.

Most pastas take five to six hours to dry, but long, thick pastas can take much longer. Long pastas are usually hung to dry in long sheets. This helps keep their flat shape. After they are dry, they are cut to the desired size.

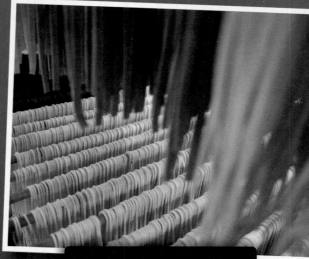

Spaghetti is hung to dry.

Imagine a company that makes both short and long pastas. The short pasta makes up $\frac{2}{5}$ of all the pasta. Eight different shapes of short pasta, including wheels, are made in equal amounts. To find the fraction of wheels in the pasta produced, divide $\frac{2}{5}$ by 8. Think of a box that represents the pasta made by the company. The box has 5 rows and 8 columns.

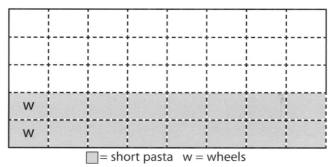

□ = short pasta   w = wheels

$$\frac{2}{5} \div 8 \text{ is the same as } \frac{2}{5} \div \frac{8}{1}$$

Step 1: Multiply by the **reciprocal**.

Step 2: Simplify.

$$\frac{2}{5} \times \frac{1}{8} = \frac{2}{40}$$
$$\frac{2}{40} = \frac{1}{20}$$

Wheels make up $\frac{1}{20}$ of the pasta produced.

Notice that dividing by 8 is equivalent to multiplying by $\frac{1}{8}$.

Packaging is one of the final steps in manufacturing foods. A computer weighs the right amount of pasta for each package. Cellophane (SEL-uh-feyn) bags are sometimes used to package pasta. They protect the pasta from moisture and insects. Boxes are also used. They are easy to shelve, and they protect pasta from breaking. Also, it is easy to read the information printed on the box.

Pasta is packaged in $2\frac{1}{2}$-pound boxes. One-eighth of a pound of dry pasta is considered one serving. How many servings of pasta are in a $2\frac{1}{2}$-pound box?

Each bar represents one pound of pasta. It is divided into eighths to show the serving size.

We are looking for the number of $\frac{1}{8}$-pound servings in $2\frac{1}{2}$ pounds of dry pasta. Notice that $2\frac{1}{2}$ bars are shaded. Count the $\frac{1}{8}$-pound portions. There are 20 servings.

$2\frac{1}{2} \div \frac{1}{8}$

$2\frac{1}{2} \times \frac{8}{1}$

$\frac{5}{2} \times \frac{8}{1}$

$\frac{40}{2}$ servings

20 servings

Notice that dividing by $\frac{1}{8}$ is equivalent to multiplying by 8.

Once dried, pasta is ready for packaging.

Improper Fractions

To simplify an improper fraction, divide the numerator by the denominator. You may get a whole number or a mixed number. If you get a mixed number, remember to simplify the fraction.

Where Did Pasta Come From?

Pasta originally came from China. The explorer and trader Marco Polo brought pasta to Italy when he returned in 1295 from a 24-year trip to Asia.

What's Next?

People who work in the food **industry** are always working on new products. As they try out new ideas, they must think about safety, cost, quality, and flavor. New food items are invented all the time! The next time you are in a grocery store, look around—you are sure to spot something new. You may find yourself wondering, *how do they make that?*

LET'S EXPLORE MATH

a. How many $\frac{1}{8}$-pound servings are in a 3-pound bag of granola?

b. How many $\frac{3}{16}$-pound servings are in $\frac{2}{3}$ pounds of rice?

c. How many $1\frac{2}{3}$-cups servings are in $7\frac{1}{2}$ cups of yogurt?

The Chip Factory

Factories must make sure that the food they produce is free of **contamination** (kuhn-tam-uh-NEY-shuhn), like insects and mold. They also must make sure that the food tastes correct. They check that it is the right size and color. Samples of the product are tested for quality.

At a potato chip factory, four bags of potato chips are pulled aside from each batch for testing. Each bag weighs 1.2 ounces.

Solve It!

a. All four bags of chips are mixed together to make a large sample. How much does the sample weigh?

b. The large sample is then divided into six smaller samples. How much does each of the six samples weigh?

c. Two-thirds of the samples are original flavor. What is the weight of the samples that are original flavor?

d. If the potato chip factory produces 100 bags of chips per batch, what is the percent of bags in each batch that are not tested?

Use the steps below to help solve the problems.

Step 1: Use repeated addition or multiplication to find the total weight of four bags of chips.

Step 2: Divide your answer for problem **a** by 6.

Step 3: Multiply your answer for problem **a** by $\frac{2}{3}$.

Step 4: Subtract the number of bags tested from the number of bags of potato chips produced. Write a fraction that shows the number of bags not tested over the total number of bags in the batch. Change the fraction to a decimal by dividing, then multiply by 100.

Glossary

apex—the top

contamination—introduction of a material that does not belong

dilute—to make a liquid thinner or weaker by adding water to it

dividend—a number to be divided

divisor—a number by which another number is divided

edible—can be eaten

endosperm—the nourishing part of the seed

equivalent—having the same value

extraction—the process of getting something by pulling or forcing it out

factors—numbers that divide exactly into another number; numbers multiplied together to get a product

greatest common factor (GCF)—the largest factor shared by two numbers

harvested—gathered, as with crops

improper fraction—a fraction whose numerator is greater than its denominator, for example $\frac{40}{2}$

industry—a group of businesses that provide a particular product or service

least common denominator (LCD)—the smallest common multiple of the denominators of two or more fractions

multiples—products of a whole number and any other whole number

percent—a part of a whole expressed in hundredths

proverbs—short, popular sayings

reciprocal—either of a pair of numbers (such as $\frac{2}{3}$ and $\frac{3}{2}$) whose product is 1

simplest form—a fraction whose numerator and denominator have no common factor greater than 1

vacuum—a space in which air and all other gasses are absent

varieties—a number of different types of things

yield—to make or produce

Index

Let's Explore Math

Page 7:

a. 39.7 pounds

b. 223.2 pounds

Page 11:

a. 66.15 grams

b. 154.35 grams

c. 154.35 grams

d. The answers are the same because a 75% increase in calories is the same as 175% of the original calories (75% = 0.75 and 175% = 1.75).

e. 130.5 grams

Page 13:

a. 44°F

b. 66°F

c. 66°F

Page 17:

a. 4%

b. 5.95%

Page 19:

a. $24\frac{1}{2}$ hours

b. $5\frac{1}{6}$ hours

Page 22:

a. $\frac{1}{2}$ ounce

b. $1\frac{1}{3}$ ounces

c. $1\frac{5}{6}$ ounces

d. $1\frac{5}{6}$ ounces; They are the same.

Page 27:

a. 24 servings

b. $3\frac{5}{9}$ servings

c. $4\frac{1}{2}$ servings

Problem-Solving Activity

a. 4.8 ounces

b. 0.8 ounce

c. 3.2 ounces

d. 96%